WILDFLOWERS

A PORTRAIT OF THE NATURAL WORLD

Andrew Cleave

TODTRI

This book was designed and produced by
Todtri Productions Limited
P.O. Box 572
New York, NY 10116-0572
Fax: (212) 279-1241

Printed and bound in Singapore

ISBN 1-57717-028-8

Author: Paul Sterry

Publisher: Robert Tod
Editorial Director: Elizabeth Loonan
Book Designer: Mark Weinberg
Senior Editor: Cynthia Sternau
Project Editor: Ann Kirby
Photo Editor: Edward Douglas
Picture Researchers: Heather Weigel, Laura Wyss
Production Coordinator: Jay Weiser
Typesetting: Command-O Design

PHOTO CREDITS
Photographer/Page Number

James H. Carmichael, Jr. 3, 4, 6, 7, 11 (bottom), 43 (bottom), 48 (top), 52, 53, 54, 55 (top), 58, 59, 60 (top), 66 (top), 67 (bottom), 68, 69, 70 (top & bottom), 71

E.R. Degginger 23, 29 (bottom), 42, 44, 50 (bottom), 55 (bottom), 56–57, 67 (top)

Phil Degginger 19 (top)

Dembinsky Photo Associates
Willard Clay 5, 14, 20, 29 (top), 63 (right)
Dan Dempster 8–9
Terry Donnelly 65
Greg Gawlowski 33 (top)
Barbara Gerlach 66 (bottom)
Darrell Gulin 36 (top), 50 (top)
Adam Jones 27, 33 (bottom)
Bill Lea 46, 47 (top)
Doug Locke 34, 41–42
Skip Moody 10, 11 (top), 24, 51
Stan Osolinski 25 (top), 30, 60 (bottom), 63 (left)
Rod Planck 19 (bottom), 28
Richard Schiell 36 (bottom), 61
Bob Sisk 39
Joe Sroka 31

Nature Photographers
Brinsley Burbridge 16, 32, 35 (top & bottom)
Robin Bush 18
Andrew Cleave 45
E.A. Janes 49
Paul Sterry 15 (bottom), 25 (bottom), 26 (bottom)

Picture Perfect 21
Gerald Cubitt 43 (top)

Tom Stack & Associates
Mary Clay 15 (top)
Ann Duncan 38
Jeff Foott 22
John Gerlach 48 (bottom)
Rod Planck 47 (bottom), 62
John Shaw 13, 17, 26 (top), 37
Doug Sokell 64

INTRODUCTION

The bright colors of the day lily (Hemerocallis fulva) attract insects. The anthers are held in just the right position to dust any insect with pollen as it pushes into the center of the flower for its reward of nectar.

Wildflowers have always been a source of inspiration to artists and poets. Flowers have appeared in some of the earliest forms of art and are referred to in many ancient texts, including the Bible. Our earliest ancestors knew how to use plants for food and medicine, but they also enjoyed the appearance and scent of the flowers themselves, using them in burials and religious rituals as well as for decoration. The ancient Egyptians practiced gardening, as did the Romans, and in Christian times the knowledge of how to use wild plants was greatly used by monastic communities.

Gardens are universally popular, but there is still a special charm and fascination with wildflowers. The cultivation and cross-breeding of wildflowers by gardeners to produce the immense variety of garden flowers we have today has been taking place for many hundreds of years. Discovering a beautiful orchid growing in a woodland glade, or spotting a delicate saxifrage growing out of an inhospitable mountain ledge high in the Alps gives a plant-hunter more of a sense of achievement than being shown the same plant growing in a garden. The sudden blooming of a desert after long-awaited rain, or the sight of a roadside adorned by wild daisies and clovers can lift the spirits. It is far more rewarding to find a wild plant growing happily in its natural environment than it is to spot its cultivated counterpart growing in a neatly kept garden—so the attraction of seeking wildflowers remains.

Happily, most people live within easy reach of places where wildflowers grow, for even in the heart of the city, the tiniest patch of waste

3

ground or neglected corner of a park will be brightened by the blooms of wildflowers. Studying wildflowers needs only a minimum of equipment. Nothing more than an observant nature is needed to start with but a small pocket magnifying glass will help identify flowers too tiny to study with the unaided eye, but it will also help the flower lover to appreciate the beauty of larger flowers.

To some people, certain wildflowers are classed as weeds. This rather derogatory term gives quite the wrong impression of some very beautiful flowers. A weed is simply a plant growing in the wrong place. It may compete with vegetables or herbs in our gardens for valuable growing space or water, or spoil the immaculate appearance of a well-tended lawn. It is still worth a close look however, for it will have flowers of its own and will be visited by insects like many other plants. It may have an interesting history, for some of the plants considered to be troublesome weeds now were once used as medicinal or culinary herbs, which is how they happened to be so common in towns and gardens. At one time, people depended on the plants around them for food, flavorings, medicine and even magic potions! Before throwing away an uprooted weed, take the time to look closely at it; studying wildflowers can begin very close to home.

Orchids have elaborate flowers, and this slipper orchid, Paphiopedilum callosum *from Southeast Asia* **shows how the petals have formed a tube like structure to enclose the anthers and stigma. A visiting insect must probe down inside the tube for nectar, and in the process will pick up the pollen.**

The deserts of Arizona are brightened by the stunning flowers of the barrel cactus. Safe from grazing animals with their protection of spines, these flowers are visited by both hummingbirds (attracted by the red color), and large insects.

ALL ABOUT FLOWERS

In order to survive a plant must have light, water, nutrients and a space to grow in. It will probably need soil, but some plants are capable of growing on the trunks of trees, floating in water, or surviving in crevices in rocks. In order to get sufficient light, plants compete with each other by growing taller or by spreading out to take up more room. The plant may also have to protect itself in some way by growing protective spines or having an unpleasant taste. Once the basic needs for life are satisfied and the plant can produce food and grow successfully, it is able to reproduce itself. This is where the flowers become important.

The Structure of the Flower

Plants do not produce elaborate flowers just for humans to admire. A considerable effort is put into the production of the flower, which may be a large and complicated structure and often has a scent and a supply of nectar. Its sole purpose is to ensure the pollination of the ovules contained inside the ovary so that fertile seeds can be formed. Pollen from one plant must be transferred to a different plant of the same species in order to fertilize the ovule, which then develops into the seed. Once pollination occurs, the flower can wither away; everything apart from the seed pod shrivels and the seeds continue their development inside a seed pod. Annual plants, which complete their life-cycle in the space of one year, will die away completely, leaving only their seeds to survive the winter.

In order to transfer the pollen from one flower to another, plants have evolved an immense range of shapes, sizes, colors and scents in their flower structures; these are primarily designed to attract pollinating insects, which are tempted to visit the flower by the prospect of a meal of nectar, and, in the process, become dusted with pollen. The pollen itself is a source of food for many species and is carried away in large quantities by bees that have specially formed pollen baskets on their legs to help them. When they visit the next flower, the pollen is

Look deep inside the flower and the important structures which help its reproduction will be revealed. Inside the circle of petals is a ring of anthers which release a fine dust of yellow pollen grains. Inside this lies the stigma, the female part of the flower, which receives pollen from another plant before producing seeds.

The banana passion-flower (Passiflora mollissima) of Colombia, is pollinated by hummingbirds that cannot help but be dusted with pollen as they probe their beaks down into the base of the flowers for a drink of nectar. The anthers and the stigma are close together, so that pollen stuck to the head of the hummingbird will be transferred to the stigma of the next flower it visits.

carried with them and deposited. Both the flowers and the insects have evolved together to ensure that pollination takes place; the flowers have a huge range of sizes and shapes, many of them designed for a particular species of insect. The orchids probably show the best adaptations, with many species, such as the bee orchids of Europe, looking remarkably like the insects they are trying to attract.

The typical flower consists of the flower stalk topped by an arrangement of sepals and petals surrounding the reproductive organs, located inside the flower. The sepals enclose the flower bud before it opens and are usually green, but in some species—like orchids or lilies—they may be very colorful and look like petals. The petals themselves are normally the most colorful and eye-catching part of the flower. The petals vary in number, depending on the species of flower, and the number and arrangement of petals and sepals is important in the identification of individual species. As the flower opens and the petals spread out, the sepals usually wither away. Inside the ring of petals lie the male and female reproductive organs. The male part of the flower is the anther, which produces pollen; most flowers have many anthers, normally yellow in color and positioned in such a way that insects will come into contact with them when they visit the flower. The female part of the flower is the ovary, topped by the stigma, which is sticky so pollen grains will adhere to it. Inside the ovary are one or more ovules, which eventually form the seeds.

There is a huge variety of forms of flower structure, with endless variation in the color, shapes and sizes of flowers, each one showing a particular adaptation to its environment. Most flowers contain both male and female reproductive organs, but in some species the sexes are separate. In a few species self-pollination is possible, but, for most plants, pollen must be transferred from one to another.

Flower Shape and Structure
The shape of the flower is very important in the pollination process, since there would be no benefit in offering a free meal of nectar if the visiting insect did not carry away the pollen to the next flower it landed on. In order to get to the nectar, the insect

A ruby-throated hummingbird hovers in front of a trumpet flower, sipping nectar delicately through its long beak. As it pushes further inside the trumpet, its head will become dusted with pollen. Trumpet flowers have long tubes that prevent insects from reaching the nectar, but still allow hummingbirds to do so.

usually has to push its head deep down inside the flower and extend its tongue, or even crawl right inside the flower, so that it can reach the nectar. The anthers, which produce the pollen, are positioned in such a way that they will come into close contact with the insect's body and deposit the pollen grains. These are microscopic structures that look like a fine yellow dust to the unaided eye, are slightly sticky, and easily adhere to the hairs on the insect.

When the insect arrives at the next flower it may pick up more pollen, or, if the flower is in a different stage of development, the pollen grains will be brushed off and stick to the stigma. This is the tip of the female part of the flower, which contains the ovules, or unfertilized seeds. When in contact with the stigma, the pollen grain produces a minute thread-like structure, which grows down into the ovary and fertilizes the ovules. Once this happens, seed development begins, thus the main function of the flower has been achieved.

The Importance of Color

The colors of wildflowers are a delight to human eyes, but they are there for an important reason. Many wildflowers are white or yellow, especially those which open early in the year. These colors are easy for insects to see, contrasting with the green foliage surrounding them. Human eyes are unable to detect light in the ultraviolet part of the spectrum, but insects such as honey bees are able to see this, and, through their eyes, flowers that may appear to be white or yellow to us have a darker center or a pattern indicating where the nectar is to be found. Another common range of colors in wildflowers is the blue, purple or pink part of the spectrum, which often appears in flowers that bloom later in the year. Again, these colors are easy for insect eyes to detect.

The simple flowers of the round-lobed hepatica (Hepatica americana) from the eastern United States are especially attractive to bees, which are able to detect colors in the blue range of the spectrum. White anthers create a contrasting center to the flowers, making them an easy target for insects in flight.

Honey bees work their way around the tiny florets in the center of a composite flower, which can provide them with a useful meal of nectar as well as pollen they can use to make wax. Bright colors and patterns not visible to the human eye, attract honey bees to flowers rich in nectar.

In both the North and South American continents, there is a higher proportion of red flowers than in other parts of the world. Red is a color more easily detected by birds, so this is an aid to the pollination of flowers by hummingbirds, which are found only on these continents, and not elsewhere. At least ten percent of the native wildflowers in North and South America are pollinated by hummingbirds. These flowers have a rather different structure than insect-pollinated flowers; they are normally held out away from the plant and droop downwards, so a hovering hummingbird can more easily insert its bill to reach the nectar. The Christmas cactus of Mexico or the fuchsia *(Fuchsia)* of Argentina are good examples of hummingbird-pollinated flowers.

The shape and position of bird-pollinated flowers usually make it very difficult for insects to get at the nectar or pollen, although a small number of large moths are able to hover in front of the flower and insert their tongues deep inside them.

The treasure flower (Gazania nivea), from South Africa, is a composite flower, made up of many tiny florets clustered together. Each floret can produce pollen and make seeds. Together, they make an eye-catching display that attracts the attention of distant insects. When an insect arrives, the striking pattern on the petals guides it to the nectar and pollen.

Scent

In addition to the visual attraction of the petals, many flowers produce a scent to guide the insects in. This may be a pleasant, sugary sweet scent, which people also find attractive, or it may be a foul, rotting flesh scent that attracts scavenging insects, such as flies and wasps. Some flowers release their scent only at night, so night-flying insects, like moths, will be attracted to them. The moths have long flexible tongues that can extend deep down inside the flowers to reach the nectar, which remains safe from smaller insects during the day.

A single flower will attract pollinating insects, but a mass of flowers is an even greater attraction. Some plants produce their flowers individually, but grow in groups to increase the visual attraction, whereas other plants produce many blossoms on the same plant to make a greater impression. Many tiny flowers clustered together are just as likely to attract a bee as a single large bloom. The flower of a daisy or thistle is, in fact, a collection of many, sometimes hundreds, of individual small florets clustered together in a compact flower head to look like an individual blossom. These composite flower heads are worth a closer look through a magnifying glass, for each tiny individual floret is a miniature flower. Some are called ray florets and are found around the outside of the flower, bearing what appear to be the petals, and others are disc florets, which form the central part of the flower and bear no petals. From a distance, a composite flower looks like a conventional arrangement of petals and sepals, but, on closer examination, they are seen to be very complex structures.

Other Aids to Pollination

Not all flowers are pollinated by insects. Some rely on the wind to do the job for them, so they have no need for colorful petals, elaborate flower structures or strong scents. Their floral structure is normally reduced to an absolute minimum so the wind can easily blow the pollen away. Petals and sepals are absent, but the male and female reproductive organs are still present. The anthers are usually more numerous and delicate, so they can easily be shaken around by the wind to release the pollen.

Plants that depend on the wind for pollenation produce more pollen, which is smooth rather than sticky and blows away easily. This type of pollen fills the air in summertime, making life miserable for those people suffering from hay fever, who breathe in the pollen grains every time they go outdoors. Many trees are wind pollinated, as well as many grasses and cereals, which cover huge areas of the land. Although their flowers are greatly reduced in size, they have a beauty of their own and are worth a closer look with a magnifying glass. Observe the nodding heads of grass flowers or the delicate catkins of willow trees, whose tiny flowers can be seen to have a wonderful range of forms and colors.

Where Wildflowers Grow

Anyone who travels through the countryside will notice striking changes in the growth of plants from one area to another. The plants of a shady woodland are quite different from those growing on the margins of a lake, and the wildflowers found on open grassy plains are nothing like those flourishing on cliffs or dunes beside the sea.

On a wider scale, the plants of a desert bear very little resemblance to those of a tropical forest, so there must be a reason for the great variation in plant form seen in the different habitats. Each plant is suited to its environment and will only grow there if it can cope with the special conditions of that area. The spiny drought-resistant plants of a desert have evolved to cope with hot, intensely bright sunlight and lack of water, whereas the scrambling woody vines (called lianas) of tropical forests have adapted to cope with the shade and humidity of the interior of a dense forest.

A few species of plants are very widespread and can grow in several different habitats, but most are suited to one habitat only. Part of the delight of searching for wildflowers is the anticipation of finding a particular species in the correct place; knowing that a mountain ledge is the place to search for a rare saxifrage makes it all the more rewarding when the plant is finally discovered.

A colorful carpet of arnica and fleabane in a Colorado meadow in August is a delight to human eyes and enlivens a summer walk in the countryside. Sights like this are mostly confined to poor land, as much of the rich land where they once grew has now been plowed.

MOUNTAIN FLOWERS

Some of the most extreme climatic conditions on Earth are found in high mountainous regions, which are characterized by long periods of temperatures well below freezing point, severe winds, high rainfall, deep blankets of snow, soils lacking in plant nutrients, or even no soil at all. Despite these conditions, there are many beautiful wildflowers to be found growing high up in the mountains at the very limit of the snow and ice.

Alpine Flowers

The thick blanket of snow that covers high mountains in winter prevents any plant growth from taking place, but it also acts as a protection from the most severe of the winter conditions. Icy winds and temperatures well below freezing are common conditions on high mountains, but beneath the snow blanket the plants are sheltered from this and can remain dormant until the spring sun melts the snow.

A few flowers seem unable to wait for the snow to disappear completely and burst into life at the edge of the retreating snow blanket; the delicate alpine snowbell *(Soldanella pusilla)* pushes its single flower spike through the snow, its tiny purple-pink blossoms contrasting vividly with the chilly surroundings. Some insects may also emerge early in the year, pollinating flowers as they search for food. As the snow retreats further, the leaves of the alpine snowbell are uncovered and the tiny plant can then set seed and produce a new set of leaves for the following year.

Most alpine flowers must wait until the snow has retreated fully before they can produce their flower spikes. The mountain avens

Alpine meadows, such as this scenic setting in Colorado, are filled in summer with a lush growth of grasses and flowering plants and provide rich grazing. Bees also make use of the flowers and for a time in summer, mountain slopes are colorful with the flowers, filled with their scent and alive with sounds of insects.

Snow buttercups (Ranunculus adoneus) live up to their name, flowering happily through a thin blanket of snow. Amongst the first of the alpine flowers to open in the spring, they provide a welcome splash of color in the high mountains as the winter snows recede.

Purple lupins dominate the view in Glacier National Park, Alaska. Tolerant of very severe conditions, lupins can grow well where other plants would fail, and they actually help improve the soil fertility. Their flowers have a strange peppery scent, and only heavyweight bees are strong enough to push inside them to reach the nectar.

(Dryas integrifolia) utilizes the sun's rays to warm up the center of the flower, where the pollen and seeds form, by turning its head around to follow the sun's progress through the sky during the day. The eight white petals act as a solar reflector, concentrating the warmth of the sun into the center of the flower. In the arctic, where the sun may be above the skyline for a full twenty-four hours, the mountain avens can make good use of the very brief arctic summer

Life in a Cold Climate

Alpine flowers are adapted to life in extremely cold conditions and most can cope with very poor soils, or even no soil at all in some cases, but they are usually unable to tolerate long periods of exposure to wet weather. In winter, they are normally protected under snow, and at other times of year, when there may be heavy rainfall, they cope by having an arrangement of leaves that encourages the water to run off and not collect around the base of the plant. Summer rainfall usually evaporates very quickly.

Alpine flowers that have been transplanted into lowland gardens, where they experience higher temperatures, richer soils and competition from other plants, do not normally grow as well as they do in the extreme conditions of a mountain. A typical mountain flower has a deep tap root and a low-growing rosette, or cushion of small leaves, to minimize the surface area it exposes to the weather. The leaves themselves often are covered in grayish silky hairs, or they have a waxy coating in order to conserve water, which can be scarce on exposed rock faces.

The flowers on most alpines are produced on a flower spike, which emerges from the rosette in summer. If this is damaged by severe weather or eaten by a grazing animal, the rest of the plant is not affected, and, although it will probably not produce another flower spike in that year, it will try again in the next growing season. Most alpine flowers are very slow growing, long-lived plants that are tolerant of severe weather, but, unfortunately, not safe from the trowels of collectors!

Mount Teide on the Canary Islands has many endemic flowers, found nowhere else in the world. A large endemic Echium wildprettii *raises long spikes of tiny flowers into the air to attract the limited number of pollinating insects that live at high altitude.*

In their wild state, lupins are predominantly purple in color, but horticulturists have cultivated them to produce a range of colors not normally seen in nature.

In addition, many alpine flowers adopt other means of reproducing if the growing season is so poor that they are unable to set seed. Most are very slow growing, perennial plants, so they are able to try again another year if one season is unsuitable. Some are able to form tiny bulbils on the stems, which can drop off the plant and grow when they land in a suitable place. Others may send out long runners that terminate in buds and roots; these can plant themselves in a new spot some distance from the parent plant.

Saxifrages

Of all the flowers that live on the mountains, the saxifrages (Saxifragaceae) are best-suited to life in harsh conditions. Their name gives a clue to their suitability for living on mountains, since saxifrage literally means the rock-splitter. Many of them appear to grow directly out the solid rock, forming rosettes, or compact cushions of tightly packed leaves with delicate flowers, often on long spikes, emerging from the leaf cushion. Most have a deep tap-root, which anchors the plant and penetrates down into a rock crevice in search of water.

Able to grow out of the bare rock, the saxifrages can survive in places where other plants would be quite unable to flourish, so they suffer no competition for space or light. They are also usually safe from the attentions of grazing animals, like chamois or mountain sheep, which, although very agile, cannot normally reach plants on vertical surfaces. The saxifrages are among the most popular of all the alpine plants with gardeners, because they take well to cultivation and thrive on neglect!

Mountain Ledges

Mountain ledges can often be filled with a lush assembly of flowers, grasses and ferns. At first, a narrow rocky ledge is colonized by a few hardy mosses and saxifrages, which can survive with a minimum of soil and nutrients.

The Water Saxifrage, (Saxifraga aquatica) grows beside a stream in the Spanish Pyrenees, living up to the name of the 'rock breaker' plants by growing out of a narrow rock crevice where it finds a secure attachment for its roots.

Safe from grazing animals, they grow and reproduce, and, after a few years, these first colonizers succeed in creating the conditions that permit other flowers to gain a foothold.

Gradually, a whole colony of alpine flowers will build up on what was once an exposed rock ledge. After many years of growth, a dense mass of vegetation and rich organic matter called humus may accumulate on the ledge; it may become so dense that, after a period of heavy rain, it will fall off the ledge under its own weight and land at the bottom of the cliff. Some plants may survive here, but others may be grazed by sheep. Meanwhile, back on the ledge the whole process begins again, with the bare rock being colonized by the hardiest of the mountain flowers.

The stonecrop (Sedum cauticolum) has fleshy leaves that are resistant to dry conditions, so that if its rocky habitat suffers from drought conditions it can retain enough water to flower late in the summer. Like other stonecrops, it has red flowers that are extremely popular with insects, especially butterflies.

The tiny but colorful Mexican fleabane (Erigeron mucronatus) grows out of a rock crevice. So successful is it at colonizing rock faces by means of its wind-dispersed seeds that it has spread to towns and cities where it finds root-holds in walls and buildings.

A shrub of mountain laurel in Great Smoky Mountains National Park, United States, grows out of streamside rock crevice. Many mountain plants are able to cope with difficult growing conditions, surviving on a minimum of soil, often producing beautiful flowers despite the harsh environment.

A wealth of colorful wildflowers bloom radiantly in the French countryside. The flowers blooming on this sunny riverbank are undoubtedly quite different from those that grow on the snow-capped mountains in the distance.

Meadows and Riverbeds

Below the steepest cliffs and crags lie rich pastures; the soil forms from the eroded rocks from the cliffs above and is often rich in nutrients, which have been dissolved out of the mountain itself by the high rainfall. The alpine meadows are spectacular in summer, when a wealth of wildflowers and grasses come into flower. Wild orchids (Orchidaceae), buttercups *(Ranunculus)*, pasque flowers *(Anemone)*, gentians (Gentianaceae) and meadowsweets *(Filipendula)* are just a few of the colorful species that enrich these pastures with a breathtaking display of color. The flowers attract bees and butterflies, which further enliven the pastures, and many of them are highly prized as grazing lands for cattle, which are brought up from their winter quarters in the lowlands to spend the summer feeding on the rich grasses.

The stony beds of mountain rivers are often good places for searching for mountain flowers, since plants that have been dislodged by rock falls or erosion high up in the mountain are carried along by mountain streams and eventually deposited on shingle banks in the river valley. They may grow here for a while until a further flood washes them away completely. Care should be taken when searching for plants in river beds, because a sudden storm in the mountains could lead to a flash flood washing down the river. If the mountain plants are washed away to the lowlands, they probably will not survive for very long, being unable to cope with competition from more vigorous plants.

Tundra

Similar conditions to those found on high mountains can also be experienced in the polar regions, and some of the flowers of higher altitudes can be seen growing almost at sea level in the far north of Canada, Greenland and Siberia. The climate can be even more severe here, where long dark winters, prolonged spells of freezing winds and low rainfall lead to the formation of an arid landscape known as a polar desert.

The strong winds of the tundra may carry tiny ice crystals along, which can erode rocks and damage plants, so only the toughest species can grow here. Even in a polar desert, however, the mountain avens and the tufted saxifrage may flourish, packing all of the

growing and reproduction into the short arctic summer. For a very brief period, the tundra blossoms in the perpetual daylight and the few insects that can live here busily pollinate the flowers, which do manage to open when the sun warms them sufficiently.

Despite the low level of rainfall, the tundra can be very wet in summer due to the melting of the permafrost, the layer of frozen ground just below the surface. As it melts it forms vast areas of shallow pools, which are adorned with the fluffy white heads of cotton grass and are favored breeding grounds for midges. Only the surface melts, however, for underneath the top layer is a thick layer of ice that never melts and acts as an impenetrable barrier to plant roots.

Moss campion, (Silene acaulis), *growing here high up on a scree slope in the Glacier National Park, Alaska, is a very common mountain plant and one which can grow at very high altitudes, and far to the north where the summers are very short. Its compact cushion of leaves and short-stemmed flowers help it conserve moisture and protect it from severe weather.*

Animals avoid eating the highly poisonous azure monkshood (Aconitum carmichaelii), *but it does provide a good meal of nectar for bees clever enough to find their way inside the complex flower.*

WILDFLOWERS OF WAYSIDES AND WOODLANDS

It is often the familiar plants, seen every day as we travel to work or sit in the garden that are overlooked and taken for granted. Perhaps when they suddenly vanish for some reason they are missed for the first time. Not everyone stops to look at the wildflowers growing alongside a path, for they are not always large and conspicuous, but many of them are very beautiful to look at, especially if studied through a small magnifying glass.

Many of the most common wildflowers are adapted to life in disturbed places. They may be annuals—which produce huge numbers of seeds—growing in a garden, or plants that can survive regular mowing and trampling growing in lawns. They may have wind-dispersed seeds that get carried to a whole range of new habitats, or tough and resistant roots and stems, which help them survive the pollution of towns and cities. Whatever the reasons for them living there, they bring a welcome touch of color and a breath of country air to the center of town.

A Different Kind of Traveler

Some plants travel along roads and highways, their seeds being dispersed by the rush of traffic or carried along on the coats of animals. When the first European settlers arrived in North America, they unintentionally brought the seeds of several species of plants with them, which managed to grow alongside the native wildflowers. Some of the introduced species died out very quickly, unable to cope with the different climate and soils, but many more grew very successfully and are now, three hundred years later, very well-established and flourishing. Broad-leaved plantain (genus *Plantago*) and purple loosestrife *(Lythrum salicaria)* now seem to be far more abundant in their new homes than in their native lands.

The beautiful yellow lady's slipper orchid (Cypripedium calceolus) has disappeared from many areas as collectors have taken it from the wild to grow in their gardens. Given special protection, it can still be seen in open woodlands in limestone areas in Europe.

Fireweed (Chamaenerion angustifolium) is a common and widespread wildflower, considered a weed by some, but it is a good colonizer of burnt or damaged ground, hence its common name. Seen here in its wild state in Yellowstone National Park, it is just as likely to turn up on a roadside in Europe or a busy building site in a large city.

Kidney vetch (Anthyllis vulneraria) covers a sunny bank alongside an English road where it attracts not only bees to pollinate it, but small blue butterflies whose caterpillars feed on its leaves. This relative of the clovers thrives in chalky soils and is an important feature of summer pastures.

A pleasant color combination results from these fleabanes (Erigeron philadelphicus) and potentillas (Pontentilla canadensis) growing together in a summer meadow. Mixed groupings often occur in nature, and these color schemes are sometimes imitated by gardeners.

An English oakwood in spring is a delightful scene when the woodland floor is covered with bluebells (Endymion non-scriptus). Most common in England, this bulbous plant often forms a complete carpet of blue in ancient woodlands, filling the evening air with a delicate scent, but it may also be found on fern-covered mountainsides and sea cliffs around the British coast.

The combination of purple and yellow is quite common in wildflowers, as these colors are well suited to the eyesight of insects—especially honey bees—who can easily spot flowers like these leafy asters growing at Curecanti National Recreation Area, Colorado.

On the Forest Floor

The cool shade of a woodland prevents many wild plants from growing on the woodland floor, but some are suited to these conditions. Much of the greenery below the tree canopy is made up of ferns, mosses and liverworts, plants which do not bear flowers but reproduce by means of spores and thrive in damp and shady conditions. Among them, however, there are flowering plants adapted to the shade.

Several species of orchid can flower in dense shade, and the parasitic plants, which have no green leaves and rely on other plants for their food, have no problem growing here. The most dense woodland shade is cast by coniferous trees; they never lose their leaves, so the shading is permanent. The carpet of fallen needles covers the soil with a dense, sometimes resinous layer that makes growing conditions difficult and the trees themselves often grow so close together that competition for space is a problem.

It is only when a large tree falls, creating a gap in the canopy which allows sunlight through, that seedlings of wildflowers and small trees can really become established. For

A typical temperate region woodland floor scene in spring will include violets, dandelions and fern fronds. Protected during the winter by a carpet of last year's fallen leaves, the spring sun and rain will stimulate them into a new season's growth which must be completed before the leaf canopy closes over in the summer.

Early spring sunlight encourages a growth of wildflowers on the woodland floor and the bleeding heart (Dicentra spectabilis), or dutchman's breeches, comes into flower before the leaf canopy overhead has become too dense to allow sunlight to penetrate.

A carpet of large white trilliums (Trillium grandiflorum) herald spring in a woodland. Both leaves and flowers take advantage of the spring sunlight which can penetrate the upper tree canopy before the leaves are fully open. If they are unable to manage to set seed due to a late spring or poor weather, they can produce bulbous shoots from the base of the plant, making their colonies densely packed.

a while, the clearing in the forest becomes dappled with sunlight and filled with the color of flowers, but, in time, the tree canopy closes in again and the sunny patch of woodland floor becomes too shady for most plants to grow in.

Deciduous Forests

A deciduous forest, such as those found in the temperate regions, provides better growing conditions for wildflowers, since there is always a time in the year when the trees have no leaves. Before the trees produce their new set of leaves in early summer, enough light and warmth reach the woodland floor to stimulate the growth of a host of spring flowers.

An English woodland in spring is a spectacular sight, for a succession of wildflowers open up in the warm spring sunshine. Snowdrops *(Galanthus nivalis)* and hellebores *(Helleborus)* are the first to open, but of all the spring woodland flowers the bluebell is one of the most striking, usually growing in vast carpets of deep blue flower spikes. The bluebell remains hidden for much of the year, surviving underground as a bulb. In early spring, fresh green leaves emerge, followed by the

The glades morning glory (Ipomoea sagittata) *uses twining stems to clamber over other plants to reach the light, and place its beautiful flowers in the best position to attract insects as they open fully early in the day.*

A patch of wild blue phlox (Phlox divaricata) *in Great Smoky Mountains National Park makes use of early spring sunshine and a gap in the tree cover to flower early in the season. Like many other attractive wildflowers, phlox has found its way into gardens and may be familiar to some people as a cultivated plant.*

The pasque flower (Pulsatilla rubra), related to buttercups and anemones, earned its English name through its habit of flowering at Easter time. Open grassy pastures exposed to full sun are its favored habitat, and its poisonous leaves protect it from grazing sheep and rabbits.

curved flower spikes bearing their deep blue bell-shaped flowers. Often, they grow to the exclusion of all else, even covering paths and tracks. For a week or so the woodland floor mirrors the sky, but, eventually, the colors fade as the spring sun gets stronger and the leaf canopy overhead becomes thicker. Soon, all that is left are be the yellowing leaves and the seed pods filled with angular shiny black seeds. The bluebells, like so many other spring woodland flowers, make use of the time before the leaf canopy thickens up to complete their life cycle before returning to dormancy for another year.

Many other species of woodland wildflowers have a similar life cycle, concentrating all their efforts into a brief period of activity in spring. There are other woodland flowers that find places where the sunlight reaches the woodland floor, such as alongside a track, or in a clearing created by a fallen tree. They can grow well here, but if uprooted from a wood and planted out in the open they usually will not thrive. The protection from the wind or the strongest rays of the sun offered by the trees is necessary for their survival. At the height of the summer the leaf canopy overhead is at its most dense, and the plant life on the woodland floor is restricted to clearings, paths and patches of less dense canopy.

By the autumn, however, the trees start to lose their leaves, the canopy becomes thinner

California poppies (Eschscholtzia californica) and red owl's clover (Trifolium pratense) form a breathtaking spectacle in Antelope Valley, California, where a mass flowering after the rains covers a whole hillside with color. Synchronized flowering like this is an important strategy for wildflowers as pollination is far more likely to take place when many flowers bloom in the same place at the same time.

Yellow woodland sunflowers (Helianthus strumosus) brighten up a bank in a woodland glade in Great Smoky Mountains National Park, United States. By growing together in a colorful colony, the plants greatly increase their chances of attracting pollinating insects.

The wild narcissus (Narcissus rupicola) *is a common spring flower in Spain and Portugal, where spring comes early and plants have to make use of the early rains and cool conditions before the dry heat of the Mediterranean summer sets in. Many forms of Narcissus have been taken into cultivation and they are familiar plants in gardens and florists shops everywhere, but they are still a great delight when found growing in the wild.*

Swedish botanist Carl Linnaeus is said to have fallen to his knees in delight at his first sight of an English heathland where the gorse (Ulex europaeus), *was in full bloom. Sometimes covering huge areas, this very prickly shrub makes a spectacular sight as its yellow flowers grow in profusion. A scent of coconut can be detected when close to this plant, a common and widespread member of the pea family.*

Purple coneflowers (Rudbeckia) *have found their way into gardens because of their eye catching flowers. The purple coloration is particularly attractive to bees, and as with many composite flowers, the tiny disc florets in the center produce a good supply of nectar that bees can reach with their long tongues.*

A young swallow is an unusual visitor to these daisies (Erigeron sp), *finding the large disc florets a safe resting place after its first attempts to learn to fly.*

Tall spikes of foxgloves (Digitalis pur-purea) reach upwards in a woodland clearing, each spike bearing large numbers of tubular flowers. Opening from the bottom of the spike upwards, the display can last for many days. Each flower is protected by tiny hairs so that only large bumble bees can enter to reach the nectar.

The open pastures of the Texas Hill country are the ideal habitat for great sweeps of bluebonnets or lupins and the red flower heads of phlox.

and more light penetrates to the woodland floor once more. For most of the wildflowers, the growing season has long since finished, but a few species, such as the autumn crocus, burst into bloom before the winter sets in. In the autumn, the true glory of a deciduous woodland is the blaze of rich colors seen in the leaf canopy as leaf fall progresses. The leaves lose their shades of green and progress through a series of rich hues before falling to the woodland floor. Here, the earthworms take over, burying and feeding on some of the leaves and helping to enrich the soil by forming them into a humus. The loose carpet of leaves protects the dormant bulbs and tubers buried beneath the woodland floor from the cold of winter, and the humus formed by the earthworms provides the nutrients needed to help their regrowth in the following spring.

On Cultivated Soil

Forests that have been cleared are sometimes replaced by farmland on which a limited range of crops grows. Most native plants in a region are prevented from growing in order to make the best use of the land. Some wild plants are remarkably resilient, however, and a few examples of native plants often survive in neglected corners of farms or alongside tracks. If an area is left uncultivated, the dormant seeds of wildflowers germinate and take the place of the crops, and, for a while, the land looks as it did before it was farmed.

Areas of land with soil too poor to support forests or insufficient rainfall to maintain good tree growth are often covered with a

The glacial or trout lily (Eryth-roni-um grandiflorum) hangs its head in order to protect the internal structures from harsh weather conditions, especially spring rain which would soon damage the anthers and water-log the pollen.

Red poppies (Papaver sp) brighten a grassy bank in Colorado, but this scene could be found in many parts of the world where poppies are common. Their seeds can lie dormant in the soil for years; when the ground is disturbed, by plowing or road-building for example, they quickly germinate and provide a cheerful display, often disappearing as quickly as they appeared.

growth of grasses and wildflowers. At one time, huge expanses of the United States were covered with plant-rich prairies on which herds of buffalo grazed. Gradually, at first, and then at a much faster rate, much of the most fertile land was plowed so that cereal crops could be grown, and the prairie plants, and most of the animals that fed on them, almost disappeared. A few areas, mostly those too poor and stony to be cultivated, remained untouched, and these are a colorful reminder of what the great plains once looked like. Africa has great expanses of grassland where grazing animals still roam, but these areas are also diminishing under the advances of agricultural land and the southwards advance of the Sahel desert.

Following page: Far below the towering redwoods of the Redwood National Park, California, in the semi-shade of giant trees, conditions favor the growth of shrubs like the rhododendron which can tolerate low light levels, but require damp conditions and shelter from severe weather.

COASTS AND WETLANDS

Plants growing by the sea must be able to cope with drying winds, salt spray, shifting sands and poor soils, which are all found on stretches of the coast. Many coastal flowers are very hardy and at the same time very beautiful when in bloom.

Coastal Flowers

South African carpetweeds (Mesembryanthemum), now introduced to many other coastal regions around the world, have cactus-like flowers, which are produced in profusion when they grow in full sunlight. Their mat-like mass of succulent foliage and fibrous roots have made them popular plants for protecting eroded soils and cliffs and they can now be found around many stretches of the European coastline. The shifting sands of sand dunes are colonized by many annual and biennial plants, which are able to cope with the most arid of conditions.

Environmental Adaptations

The extremes of temperatures in sand dunes and the closeness of the sea lead to heavy dew formation at night, and it is this moisture that enables most small dune plants to grow so well. Many sand dune and shingle ridge plants have very extensive root systems, which penetrate far down into the sand or shingle in search of water. These root systems are often very important in stabilizing the shifting sands and creating the conditions that enable other plants to grow. The leaves of sand dune plants have waxy surfaces or deep folds, which reduce water loss and help them to survive in these extreme conditions. Tiny pansies (viola tricolor hortensis) and storksbills (Erodium) can grow among the

A drift of ice plants (Mesembryanthemum crystallium) *grow amongst granite rocks on the Monterey Peninsula, California, thriving in conditions where other plants may suffer from salt spray in winter and lack of water in summer.*

The yellow daisy (Didelia carnosa) grows across the bay from Table Mountain and Cape Town, South Africa, on a stretch of sandy shore. Like many coastal wildflowers, it has leaves covered with silky-grey hairs that help it conserve water.

The beach morning glory (Ipomoea stolonifera) earned its name from its ability to grow on sandy beaches where other plants would suffer from the salty conditions. Its seeds can float in the sea and be carried to new beaches where they germinate freely. Also known as the railroad vine flower, this flower is often spread along man-made trails such as railway embankments.

trailing stems of marram grass and beach vines and make use of the shelter provided by the more dominant plants.

A special feature of some coastal wildflowers is their ability to produce floating seeds that can survive for long periods in salt water. The sea kales (Crambe maritima) and sandworts (Arenaria) of some northern shores, and some of the beach vines of warmer regions growing just above the high tide line on sandy beaches all produce seeds that drop on to the beach and then get carried away on the next high tide or storm. Many of the seeds may drift far out into the ocean and eventually sink or are eaten, but some arrive on a new shore, where they germinate and grow. Some of these drifting seeds cross whole oceans and still remain viable. The sea beans found on beaches in western Britain are carried from the shores of the Caribbean in the currents of the Gulf Stream all the way across the Atlantic Ocean.

On sheltered stretches of coastline, sedi-

ment builds up to form mudflats and salt marshes, but only a few very specialized plants can grow here. Although there is plenty of water, it is salt water and most flowering plants are unable to cope with this. Usually, just a few species dominate a salt marsh, but for a time in late summer they can make a splash of color. Sea lavenders *(Limonium)*, sandworts *(Arenaria),* and spurreys *(Spergula arvensis)* grow in European saltmarshes, and their rather gray and monotonous foliage is relieved for a time by their flowers and the pollinating insects that visit them.

Needing virtually no soil, the seaside golden rod (Solidago sempervirens) *flourishes in a rock crevice on a sheltered sea cliff.*

Sea cliffs around the British coast are the perfect habitat for the sea pink or thrift (Armeria maritima), *which forms dense green cushions of foliage topped by nodding pink flower heads. Tolerant of very tough conditions, the sea pink can also sometimes be found on mountain ledges, but it is on seaside cliffs that it really flourishes.*

Wetlands and Marshes

Permanently waterlogged ground, high acidity and low levels of nutrients make growing conditions difficult for plants that live in boggy areas. It is even more difficult for the botanists who may want to study them, since many plants grow on a quaking carpet of bog mosses that are floating over deep mires! Approach these areas with caution. If it is safe to venture out onto a bog, then there are plenty of fascinating plants to see as a reward.

Acid bogs are normally very low in the essential minerals required for healthy plant growth, so most of the plants of acid bogs have developed unusual means of supplementing their nutrients. Many of them have evolved means of catching insects in order to derive the nutrients from the decaying body of their prey. The showy pitcher plants are brightly colored and conspicuous; their leaves are folded into large pitchers in which insects become trapped. In the base of each pitcher is a pool of foul-smelling water full of drowning and decaying insects; as they break down, the nutrients in their bodies are absorbed by the plant in place of the nutrients that would normally be present in the soil.

Large leaves indicate a plant adapted to moist and shady conditions, and the white erect trillium (Trillium erectum) is in its ideal habitat growing beside a mountain stream. It would be unable to cope with a dry, sunny site.

Marsh marigolds (Caltha palustris) thrive in boggy ground where other plants would soon become waterlogged. Related to buttercups, rather than marigolds, they have large leaves that help them make use of low light levels in damp shady places.

The bizarre tubular leaf of the pitcher plant (Sarracenia purpurea) traps water, which in turn traps insects whose decaying bodies nourish the plant. Its normal habitat of acid boggy ground is low in nutrients, so the plant depends on insects in order to grow.

One of the most ancient of plants to survive to the present day, the sacred lotus (Nelumbo nucifera) grows in water, but its leaves and flowers are raised above the surface on stalks. Revered by the ancient Egyptians, the plant is still highly favored today across the wide areas of the Africa and Asia, both as a sacred plant and as a source of food.

The charming blue and white patterned flowers of the dwarf lake iris (Iris lacustris) are designed to allow only the largest of bees to enter. Seen from above, the pattern on the petals guides the insects into the center of the flower, where they need to push between the petals.

Look around any boggy area to find many examples of insect-eating plants: sundews *(Drosera)*, with glistening hairs on their red leaves; butterworts *(Pinguicula)*, with violet-like flowers and pea-green sticky leaves; bladderworts *(Utricularia)*, with gas-filled bladders beneath the water to trap water fleas; or the notorious Venus's-flytrap *(Dionaea muscipula)*, with its snapping leaves primed to trap unwary visitors. All of these insectivorous bog plants lure insects to them for food, and they also all rely on insects for pollination.

Natural Watergardens

Non-acidic wetlands contain fewer of the insectivorous plants, but have a greater range of flowers growing both in and out of the water. The shallow margins of a lake may be fringed with reeds, and growing among them are usually colorful irises *(Iridaceae)*, loosestrifes *(Lythrum)*, arums *(Arum)*, and waterplantains *(Alisma plantago-aquatica)*. Lilies rooted in the bed of the lake float their leaves and flowers on the surface and water soldiers and water hyacinths rise up from the mud to live at the surface, floating freely during the summer before sinking into the mud for the winter.

In summer, marshes can be very colorful places, and the flowers are enhanced by the insects that live around them. Many beautiful dragonflies and butterflies live near marshlands, although they probably are not the pollinators. Bees visit to pollinate the flowers and add to the activity the insects create.

Plants growing in water have the effect of slowing down any movement of the water, so silt collects around their roots and raises the level of the bed of the lake or pond. This allows more plants to grow and, eventually,

Some riversides and lake margins are very colorful in June when the yellow flag (Iris pseudacorus) *is in full bloom. Able to grow with its roots in water, it sends its spear-like leaves upwards quickly in spring, followed by the spikes of large yellow flowers.*

The water hyacinth (Eichornia crassipes). a native of Brazil, has been introduced to many other wetlands because of its attractive flowers, especially beautiful when seen in bloom on a large lake. Unfortunately, this plant is notorious for choking up waterways and when not in flower completely covers the water surface, preventing birds from swimming and other plants from receiving any light.

the dense vegetation and a build-up of silt lead to the lake becoming a swamp; the swamp, in turn, finally becomes dry land with woodland growing on it. This process may be rapid in areas where plants can grow easily in good climatic conditions, or barely noticeable in deep lakes where growing conditions are poor. The water lilies of deep open water give way to the reeds and sedges *(cyperus)* of shallow water and, eventually, the willow and alder trees of damp ground.

Still water is easier for plants to cope with than rapidly flowing water, so lakes, ponds and swamps are far richer habitats for wildflowers than rivers. Even so, a few plants can survive in rivers despite the strong currents, and during the summer a river may become choked for a time with flowering plants. A flash flood will often wash away plants rooted in the river bed, so these are usually temporary features. Rivers may also carry a great deal of silt, which clouds the water and is unable to settle because of the current. This prevents light from reaching the leaves of the plants and thus stops them growing.

One of the most beautiful water plants, the red bengal water lily (Nymphaea rubra) opens its flowers just above the water surface. After pollination water lilies produce floating seeds that drift away from the plant, slowly absorbing water until they sink to the bottom.

Rivaling any cultivated variety, the swamp rose (Rosa palustris) produces its delicate flowers freely in the swampy habitat it prefers.

EXTREME CONDITIONS

Tropical Forests

The dense shade of the interior of a tropical forest makes growing conditions difficult for flowering plants. Although the sunlight overhead may be intense, very little of it filters through the thick tree canopy to the floor of the forest, so most plants compete with each other for light by growing taller and taller and stretching upwards. For trees this is no problem, but other smaller plants have to find different means of reaching the light. Some are tolerant of shady conditions and can grow quite happily inside the forest, having large thin leaves to trap what little light energy filters down to them. However, many use the trees for support and live high up above the forest floor—with their roots attached to the trees or even growing free in the air. These plants are known as epiphytes, since they grow on the outside of other plants. They are not parasites because they do not take any nutrients from the host plants; they merely use them for support.

Orchids and bromeliads can sometimes cover some trees to such an extent that the tree itself cannot be recognized beneath the mass of flowers and foliage. Honeysuckles, vines and "strangler" figs root themselves in the ground and scramble up the tree to reach the light, and their twining stems often completely enclose the host tree's trunk. Some of the vines of South American forests produce tubular red flowers, which attract pollinating hummingbirds; their red flowers, produced rather sparingly, stand out vividly against the green background of the forest.

Bromeliads, relatives of the pineapple, are suited to life in tropical forests where they attract hummingbirds to pollinate them by producing tall spikes of brightly colored flowers. Their leaves are arranged to trap small pools of water, and many of them can grow on the branches of trees with no need for soil.

A tiny arrow-poison frog sits inside a Red Passionflower (Passiflora coccinea) in an Ecuadorian rainforest. The frog will be no help for pollination, but a visiting hummingbird, attracted by the bright red color, will inevitably get dusted with pollen.

Orchids are incredibly varied and widespread and there seems to be no end to the variety of forms and colors they can exhibit. There are many thousands of species of orchids distributed worldwide and this South American species of tree dwelling orchid (Oncydium stacyi) is but one colorful example.

Following page: Until they give themselves away by flowering, stone flowers (Lithrops sp.), remain un-detectable in a stony desert. The daisy-like flowers are very short lived in the desert heat.

Neatly tucked away inside a showy ter-restrial bromeliad head are the true flowers which are very small and inconspicuous compared with the bright red bracts that surround them.

The largest of all flowers, measuring up to 32 inches (80 centimeters) across and weigh-ing as much as 15 pounds (7 kilo-grams) is the giant rafflesia (Rafflesia arnoldi) from the jungles of Indonesia. It has a strong smell to attract flies which must enter the flower by pushing past the central disc, which con-ceals the anthers and the stigmas. The plant itself is a parasite with no green leaves of its own.

The Bromeliad Family

Plants in the bromeliad family (Bromeliaceae) are almost entirely confined to life in trees and are well-adapted to obtain their moisture from the air around them. They have spongy roots that hang down into the air and absorb moisture from the atmosphere. Their leaves trap water and funnel it into the center of the plant, where it can be absorbed. They obtain their nutrients for growth from the debris that collects on the leaves and is then absorbed into the water. The elaborate flowers of bromeliads hang like sprays in the open forest, and many of them are pollinated by birds and large moths.

Orchids are among the most highly prized of wildflowers, and many are sought after by collectors. Fortunately for the tropical forest species, most of them grow high up in the canopy and are tricky to see. Occasionally, a large tree falls down and then the community of plants living on are made visible.

A close-up view of the tropical bromeliad Tillandsia capitata *shows that its flower head consists of several individual florets surrounded by colorful bracts. The ripe anthers are seen here releasing their yellow pollen and the white stigmas protrude from between them.*

Some hummingbirds are especially adapted to visit this type of Bromeliad flower, and have beaks curved to just the right degree to reach inside for the nectar. The actual flowers are very small and protected inside the colorful bracts.

The orchids show an immense variety of colors and forms in their flowers, although they all conform to a basic plan of having three petals and three sepals. The flower can sometimes be small and insignificant, attracting insects by means of its scent, but it is usually a very elaborate structure, often mimicking an insect in an attempt to lure another of the same species to visit it. The bee orchids are the best examples, with an array of species mimicking bees, wasps and flies. The bucket orchid has an enormous flower that turns the lower lip into a fluid-filled container. This contains a fluid that bees find intoxicating. When they drink some of it, they fall into the fluid and struggle to get out. In order to escape from the flower, they must push past the reproductive organs, getting dusted with pollen in the process. Before long they will visit another flower and deposit the pollen in the same way.

The flower of the tropical orchid Paphiopedilum callosum *is a tempting prospect for a pollinating insect such as a small wasp, but it must first figure out how to reach the nectar inside the flower.*

Desert Flowers

Water is essential to all life. A desert. therefore, presents very difficult problems to plants, since rainfall may not even be an annual event, and the soil consists only of dry sand with little or no organic content. However, some plants have learned to live in these conditions and have found ways to save water, so they can tolerate high daytime temperatures, plunging night-time temperatures and intense sunlight. Usually, they have leaves that have been reduced to spines and fleshy stems, which store water in special cells. The spines act as a protection against desert animals that would find the large store of water very attractive and try to eat the plant.

One of the most noble and instantly recognizable of all cacti is the large Saguaro Cactus, most common in Arizona. Its creamy-white flowers are held high up above the desert floor where conditions are a little cooler and pollinating insects can reach them more easily.

Despite the harshness of its surroundings, the seemingly delicate desert lily (Hesperocallis undulata) manages to bloom in Joshua Tree National Park, California. The leaves are actually quite tough, with a coating that helps them save water, and the plant has a store of water in its bulb below ground level.

The fishhook barrel cactus (Ferrocactus wislizenii) *produces a colorful rosette of flowers protected by hooked spines. Pollinators such as hummingbirds will have no trouble reaching the flowers, but nibbling animals will keep well away.*

The yellow evening primrose (Oenothera brachycarpa) *shelters at the base of a rock in the Capitol Reef National Park, Utah. On first opening the flowers are a primrose yellow, but they soon fade to orange and wither away in the heat of the sun.*

One of the most attractive of the desert flowers is the bright display shown by the prickly pear (Opuntia sp.), *growing here in the Big Bend National Park, Texas. After a mass flowering the flowers are replaced by edible fruits.*

The Cactus

The typical desert plant is the cactus, which has a swollen stem and a covering of protective spines. Most true cacti occur in the deserts of Mexico, but they also grow in the deserts of the southern United States.

For much of its life a cactus grows slowly, making use of brief spells of rainfall to capture and store water for the long periods of drought. Most cacti will flower once a year, and they often produce a vivid display of elaborate flowers in a range of colors—from white through yellows and pinks to deep reds. Many of them are pollinated by hummingbirds that visit the flowers for their rich supply of nectar. Bats also visit flowers for nectar and pollen at night when the hummingbirds are roosting. The Mexican deserts are also home to the large century plant (Agave), which is reputed to grow for a hundred years and then flower once before dying. It is true that once it has flowered it then dies, but it normally does not take one hundred years for it to grow. Throughout its life it sends out tiny side-shoots from the main plant, which flourish when the parent dies.

Far away from Mexico, in the deserts of southern Africa, a different group of plants has evolved to cope with the same arid conditions. The aloes are unrelated to the *Agaves* but they are very similar in appearance and structure—with fleshy leaves, tough cuticles and colorful spikes of flowers. Many desert plants produce large numbers of seeds, which can survive in a dormant state for years, waiting for sufficient rain to fall to encourage them to germinate. When this happens, the desert suddenly becomes green as millions of seeds burst into life; they grow rapidly in the warmth and strong sunlight and they begin to flower. It is important that they all flower at the same time so they can be pollinated and set seed. The supply of water is used up very soon, and the plants shrivel in the heat. All that will survive after this are the seeds. This is a time of plenty for the animals of the desert that can eat the leaves, collect nectar from the flowers and then eat the seeds. Enough seeds will survive to ensure the next flowering of the desert when the rains return, perhaps after a gap of several years.

Waiting for the sun to come out and stimulate them to open a group of partially closed flowers of the hedgehog cactus (Echinocereus nicholii) *receive some protection from the impending rain, an unusual event in the desert that is necessary for flower production.*

The towering flower spike of the century plant (Agave americana) *reaches up into the desert sky to attract night-flying bats to pollinate it. Once it has set seed the whole plant will die, but a few shoots at the base may continue to grow into a new plant.*

Lantana flowers are a familiar sight throughout the tropics, for this colorful species has become widespread through human introduction, being planted as a garden hedge, as a specimen plant, or just naturalizing itself on waste ground.

The woolly daisy (Eriophyllum wallacei) growing in Joshua Tree National Park, California, earned its name from its gray-green woolly coat, not intended to keep it warm in the desert, but to protect the leaves from drying out in the arid conditions.

The red flowers of the peanut cactus
(Chamaecereus silvestrii) *found in Argentina,*
attract hummingbirds that pollinate it.
As the birds reach down inside the tubular
base of the flower, their heads pick up
the pollen from the ring of yellow anthers.

Imitating a bee is a good way of
encouraging one to visit you for
the purposes of pollination, and
this bee orchid (Oncidium henekenii)
from Hispaniola has evolved
to look like a specific bee species.

A Special Environment

Deserts are thought of as being barren and very hot places, but this is not always the case. Many have attractive specialized plants growing in them with associated animals depending on them, and, although very dry, some are also very cold for much of the year. Deserts may be found at sea level or very near to the sea, at high altitudes, and far inland in great continental land masses. A consequence of global warming and deforestation is an increase in the area of the world's deserts, especially in Africa. This is at the expense of grasslands and forests, so although some desert plants may become more common, many other species will be lost in the process.

Flower Mimics and Curiosities

Plants, like all living things, need food in order to survive. Most plants manufacture their own food using energy from sunlight, which they trap with chlorophyll, the green pigment in the leaves. A few species of plants live as parasites, however, obtaining their food directly from another plant. Broomrapes (Orbanchaceae) have no green leaves of their own, but they do have specially adapted roots that penetrate the root systems of other plants and tap into the supply of nutrients that the plant has produced for itself. The only major structure the broomrape does produce for itself is its flower spike, for it cannot rely on another species for reproduction. The flowers of broomrapes are very attractive structures growing on a tall spike that appears directly out of the ground. After pollination, thousands of tiny seeds are produced and are scattered around when the rather brittle flower spike is blown by the wind. The seeds must settle close to a suitable host plant so they can penetrate it with a tiny rootlet after germination. The broomrape seems to have very little effect on its host plant, which, although providing the broomrape with some food, also manages to grow

A pansy orchid (Miltonia clowesii) *from Brazil shows how one of the petals has evolved to form a tempting landing stage for an insect, while the remaining two petals and three sepals have become strikingly colored to attract the insects.*

and reproduce itself. Each species of broomrape parasitises a specific host species.

The largest flower in the world is the giant rafflesia *(Rafflesia arnoldi),* whose flowers can measure up to one meter (39 inches) across. It has a foul smell that attracts flies to pollinate it, and its tiny seeds are carried away by ants. Although it has the largest flower in the world, the Rafflesia is actually a parasite, having no green leaves of its own. Its host plant is a liana, or twining plant of rainforests, and the flower usually emerges directly from the roots on the forest floor. Sometimes it grows from a point high up in the forest where, despite its size, it is hard to see; then it is only the far-carrying smell that gives it away.

The wild arum, or cuckoo pint, also attracts insects by means of a foul smell. The flower is constructed in such a way that the insects can crawl into it but not escape until the plant is ready. The flower is actually a complex structure consisting of an outer petal-like bract or spathe, and a central column with several female flowers at the base and male flowers above them. A constriction in the neck of the spathe contains the hairs that trap the visiting insects. At the top of the central column is a colorful spike or spadix,

The carrion flower (Huernia zebrina) *earned its name from the unpleasant smell emanating from its flower. The rotting flesh odor attracts flies who transfer the pollen as they search from flower to flower for the non-existent rotting meat.*

The bizarre flower of the Colombian gesneriad (Tricantha minor) is a further example of a species which has adapted to a precise method of pollination, relying on hummingbirds with a bill long enough to reach down inside the corolla tube to pick up the pollen.

which heats up and produces the smell that attracts the flies, but plays no other part in the reproductive process. If pollination is successful, the spathe, spadix and male flowers wither away, leaving an attractive short spike of shiny red seeds.

Conservation of wildflowers

There are many threats to our wildflowers, the most serious being the loss of their habitats. This, of course, is the most serious threat to all forms of wildlife and is global in its range. No habitat is safe from man's influence, and the rate at which we are destroying these habitats is increasing rapidly. In order to preserve our wildflowers we should fight to prevent the destruction of rainforests, the pollution of oceans and shores, the draining of marshes and the contamination of the air with acid rain. By preserving habitats for wildflowers, many other forms of wildlife will also benefit. Picking wildflowers, digging them up for the garden, treating them as weeds and destroying them are not going to help their survival, but by far the most important thing to do is to guard the wild places where they grow.

The night-blooming cereus (Hylocereus undatus) from the West Indies is unusual in that it is a forest-dwelling cactus which has long triangular scrambling stems, and relies on other plants for its support. Its large fragrant flowers have given it an alternative name of queen of the night.

The hippeophyllum orchid from the forests of Malaysia has an extraordinary cylindrical flower spike which on closer examination is seen to be made up of hundreds of tiny individual flowers. Grouped together like this they make more of a spectacle and are more likely to attract pollinators.

INDEX

*Page numbers in **bold-face** type indicate photo captions.*

acid bogs, 47
adaptations to environments, 12
  by acid bog plants, 47
  by alpine plants, 16
  by bromeliads, 59
  by coastal plants, 43–44
  by desert plants, 60, 69
  by orchids, 8
  in rivers, 50
aloes, 64
alpine mountain flowers, 15–19, **15**, **16**
alpine snowbell (*Soldanella pusilla*), 15
annual plants, 7, 25
anthers, **3**, **7**, 8, 11, 12,**59**, **67,**
arnica, **12**
arums (*Arum*), 49
  wild arum (cuckoo pint), 69–70
autumn crocus, 39
azure monkshood (*Aconitum carmichaelii*), **22**

banana passion-flower (*Passiflora mollissima*), **7**
barrel cactus, **4**
bats, 64, **64**
beach morning glory (*Ipomoea stolonifera*; railroad vine), 43
beach plants, *see* coastal flowers
bee orchid (*Oncidium henekenii*), 60, **67**
bees, 7–8, 11, **35**, **48**, 49, 60
bladderworts (*Utricularia*), 49
bleeding heart (*Dicentra spectabilis*; dutchman's breeches), **29**
bluebells (*Endymion non-scriptus*), **26**, 30–32
bluebonnets, **36**
blue phlox (*Phlox divaricata*), 30
bogs, 47–48
broad-leaved plantain (*Plantago*), 25
bromeliads (Bromeliaceae), 59–60
  flowers of, **55**
  Tillandsia capitata, **59**
  in tropical forests, 53, **53**
broomrapes (Orbanchaceae), 69
bucket orchid, 60
buttercups (*Ranunculus*), 21
  snow buttercups, **15**
butterworts (*Pinguicula*), 49

cacti, 64
  barrel cactus, **4**
  fishhook barrel cactus, **63**
  hedgehog cactus, **64**
  night-blooming cereus, **70**
  peanut cactus, **67**
  prickly pear, **63**
  Saguaro Cactus, **60**
California poppies (*Eschscholtzia californica*), **33**
carrion flower (*Huernia zebrina*), 69
  giant carrion flower, **55**, 69
century plant (*Agave americana*), 64, **64**
Christmas cactus, 11
climates, *see* environments
coastal flowers, 43–44, **43**, **44**
Colombian gesneriad (*Tricantha minor*), **70**
composite flowers, **11**, 12, **35**
coniferous trees, 29
conservation of wildflowers, 70
crocus, 39
cultivated soil, 39

daisies
  Erigeron species, **36**
  woolly daisy, **66**
  yellow daisy, **43**
day lily (*Hemerocallis fulva*), **3**
deciduous forests, 30–39
desert lily (*Hesperocallis undulata*), **60**
desert plants, 12, 60, 69
  cacti, **63**, 64, **64**, **67**
  century plant, **64**
  stone flowers, **55**
  of tundra, 22
  woolly daisy, **66**
disc florets, 12
dutchman's breeches (*Dicentra spectabilis*; bleeding heart), **29**
dwarf lake iris (*Iris lacustris*), **48**

Echium wildprettii, **16**
environments
  alpine mountains, 15–19, **15**
  coastal, 43–44
  cultivated soil, 39
  deciduous forests, 30–39
  deserts, 60, 64, 69
  disturbed places, 25
  forest floor, 29–30
  meadows and riverbeds, 21
  mountain ledges, 19
  plants adaptations to, 12
  tropical forests, 53
  tundra, 22
  woodlands and marshes, 47–50
epiphytes, 53
evoluiton of flowers and insects, 8

fireweed (*Chamaenerion angustifolium*), 25
fishhook barrel cactus (*Ferrocactus wislizenii*), **63**
fleabanes, **12**
  Erigeron philadelphicus, **26**
  Mexican fleabane, **19**
floating seeds, 43–44
  of red bengal water lily, **50**
flowers
  of bromeliads, **55**, 59, **59**
  of broomrapes, 69
  of cacti, 64
  of Colombian gesneriad, **70**
  colors of, 11
  of fishhook barrel cactus, **63**
  of hippeophyllum orchid, **70**
  of orchids, 60
  of Saguaro Cactus, **60**
  of tropical orchid, **60**
  of yellow evening primrose, **63**
forests, 29–30
  bromeliads in, 59

deciduous, 30–39
  tropical, 53
foxgloves (*Digitalis purpurea*), 36
fuchsia (*Fuchsia*), **11**

garden flowers, wildflowers cross-bred with, 3
gentians (Gentianaceae), 21
giant rafflesia (*Rafflesia arnoldi*), **55**, 69
glacial Lily (*Erythronium grandiflorus*; trout lily), **39**
glades morning glory (*Ipomoea sagittata*), 30
gorse (*Ulex europaeus*), **35**
grasslands, 39

habitats of plants, 12
  loss of, 70
  see also environments
hedgehog cactus (*Echinocereus nicholii*), **64**
hellebores (*Helleborus*), 30
hepatica, **11**
hippeophyllum orchid, **70**
honey bees
  colors seen by, 11, **11**, 26
  see also bees
honeysuckles, 53
hummingbirds
  banana passion-flower pollinated by, **7**
  bromeliads pollinated by, 59
  cacti pollinated by, 64
  Colombian gesneriad pollinated by, **70**
  color of flowers and, 11
  peanut cactus pollinated by, **67**
  ruby-throated, **8**
  in tropical forests, 53

ice plants (*Mesembryanthemum crystallium*), 43
insects
  in alpine mountains, 15, **15**
  colors seen by, 26
  composite flowers pollinated by, **11**
  dwarf lake iris and, **48**
  eaten by plants, 47, **47**, 49
  in meadows, 21
  pollination by, 7–11
  scents of flowers and, 12
  of tundra, 22
introduced species, 25
  by floating seeds, 43–44
  lantana, **66**
  water hyacinth, **50**
irises
  dwarf lake iris, **48**
  Iridaceae, 49

kidney vetch (*Anthyllis vulneraria*), **25**

lantana, **66**
laurel, **20**
leafy asters, **26**
lianas, 12
lilies
  day lily, **3**
  desert lily, **60**
  glacial Lily (trout lily), **39**
  in non-acidic wetlands, 49
  red bengal water lily, **50**
  water lilies, 50
Linnaeus, Carl, **35**
loosestrifes (*Lythrum*), 49
lupins, **16**, 36
  purple lupins, **15**

marshes, 47–49
marsh marigolds (*Caltha palustris*), **47**
meadows, 21
meadowsweets (*Filipendula*), 21
Mexican fleabane (*Erigeron mucronatus*), **19**
moss campion (*Silene acaulis*), **22**
mountain avens (*Dryas integrifolia*), 15
mountain flowers, 15–19, 21
mountain ledge flowers, 19
  saxifrages, 19
  in tundra, 22
mountain laurel, **20**

narcissus, **35**
nectar, 8–11
night-blooming cereus (*Hylocereus undatus*), **70**
non-flowering plants, 29

orchids, 59–60
  adaptations by, 8
  bee orchid, **67**
  on forest floor, 29
  hippeophyllum orchid, **70**
  Oncydium stacyi, **54**
  pansy orchid, **69**
  slipper orchid, **4**
  in tropical forests, 53
  tropical orchid, **60**
  wild orchids, 21
  yellow lady's slipper orchid, **25**
ovaries, 8
ovules, 11

pansies (*viola tricolor hortensis*), 43
pansy orchid (*Miltonia clowesii*), **69**
parasitic plants, 29, 69
pasque flowers
  Anemone, 21
  Pulsatilla rubra, **32**
peanut cactus (*Chamaecereus silvestrii*), **67**
petals, 8
pitcher plant (*Sarracenia purpurea*), 47, **47**
plants
  bromeliads, 59–60
  insect-eating, 47, **47**, 49
  needs of, 7
  non-flowering, 29
  as parasites, 29, 69
  of tropical forests, 53
  as weeds, 4
polar deserts, 22

pollen, 7–8, **7**
  deposited by anthers, 11
  of wind-pollinated plants, 12
pollination
  aids to, 12
  of banana passion-flower, **7**
  of bee orchid, **67**
  of bromeliads, 59
  of bucket orchids, 60
  of cacti, 64
  of century plant, 64
  of Colombian gesneriad, **70**
  of day lily, **3**
  of fishhook barrel cactus, **63**
  by hummingbirds, 11
  of peanut cactus, **67**
  as purpose of flowers, 7
  reproductive organs for, 8
  of wetland plants, 49
  of wild arum (cuckoo pint), 69–70
potentillas (*Pontentilla canadensis*), **26**
prickly pear (*Opuntia* sp.), **63**
purple cone flowers, **35**
purple loosestrife (*Lythrum salicaria*), 25
purple lupins, **15**

railroad vine (*Ipomoea stolonifera*; beach morning glory), **43**
ray florets, 12
red bengal water lily (*Nymphaea rubra*), **50**
red owl's clover (*Trifolium pratense*), **33**
red passionflower (*Passiflora coccinea*), **53**
reeds, 50
reproductive organs of plants
  of flowering plants, 8, 11
  of non-flowering plants, 29
rhododendron, **39**
riverbeds, 21, **21**
rivers, 50
roots, 16, 43, 53, 59, 69
rosettes
  of alpine flowers, 16
  of fishhook barrel cactus, **63**
  of saxifrages, 19
round-lobed hepatica (*Hepatica americana*), 11
ruby-throated hummingbird, **8**

sacred lotus (*Nelumbo nucifera*), **48**
saguaro cactus, **60**
salt marshes, 44
sand dune plants, 43
sandworts (*Arenaria*), 43–44
saxifrages (Saxifragaceae), 19
  water saxifrage, **19**
scents of flowers, 12, **69**, **55**, 69
sea kales (*Crambe maritima*), 43–44
sea lavenders (*Limonium*), 44
sea pink (*Armeria maritima*; thrift), 44
seaside golden rod (*Solidago sempervirens*), 44
sedges (*cyperus*), 50
seeds, 7
  of desert plants, 64
  floating, 43–44, **50**
sepals, 8
shape of flowers, 8–11
slipper orchid (*Paphiopedilum callosum*), **4**
snow, 15, 16
snow buttercups (*Ranunculus adoneus*), **15**
snowcrop (*Sedum cauticolm*), 19
snowdrops (Galanthus nivalis), 30
South African carpetweeds (*Mesembryanthemum*), 43
spores, 29
spurreys (*Spergula arvensis*), 44
stigmas, 11
  of banana passion-flower, **7**
stone flowers (*Lithrops* sp.), **55**
storksbills (*Erodium*), 43
"strangler" figs, 53
structure of flowers, 7–8
  of alpine flowers, 16
  of orchids, 60
  shape and, 8–11
  of wild arum (cuckoo pint), 69–70
sundews (*Drosera*), 49
swamp rose (*Rosa palustris*), **50**
swamps, 50

thrift (*Armeria maritima*; sea pink), **44**
treasure flower (*Gazania nivea*), **11**
trillums (*Trillium grandflorum*), 29
tropical bromelaid (*Tillandsia capitata*), **59**
tropical forests, 12, 53, **53**, 59, **59**
tropical orchid (*Paphiopedilum callosum*), **60**
trumpet flowers, **8**
tundra, 22

ultraviolet light, 11

Venus's-flytrap (*Dionaea muscipula*), 49
vines, 53

watergardens, natural, 49–50
water hyacinth (*Eichornia crassipes*), 49, **50**
water lilies, 50
  red bengal water lily, **50**
waterplantains (*Alisma plantago-aquatica*), 49
water saxifrage (*Saxifraga aquatica*), **19**
water soldiers, 49
weeds, 4
wetlands, 49–49
white erect trillium (*Trillium erectum*), **47**
wild arum (cuckoo pint), 69–70
wild narcissus (*Narcissus nupicola*), **35**
wild orchids (Orchidaceae), 21
woodlands, 29–30
  see also forests
woolly daisy (*Eriophyllum wallacei*), **66**

yellow daisy (*Didelia carnosa*), **43**
yellow evening primrose (*Oenothera brachycarpa*), **63**
yellow lady's slipper orchid (*Cypripedium calceolus*), **25**
yellow woodland sunflowers (*Hellianthus strumosus*), **33**